Ransom Neutron Stars
Planting My Garden
by Stephen Rickard

Published by Ransom Publishing Ltd.
Unit 7, Brocklands Farm, West Meon, Hampshire GU32 1JN, UK
www.ransom.co.uk

ISBN   978 178591 440 9
First published in 2017

A CIP catalogue record of this book is available from the British Library.

Planting
My Garden

Stephen Rickard

Ransom

I am planting my garden.
Soon it will be summer.
Soon I will see lots
of flowers.

SEEDS

I get the seeds
for my garden.
The seeds are big.

I get my pots.
The pots are small.

I get my compost.
The compost is
good for my seeds.
The compost is in
a big bin.

I must put the compost
in the pots.
I pick up the compost.

I get rid
of the lumps
in the compost.
Lumps are not
good for seeds!

I fill the pots
with the compost.
The compost will be good
for my seeds.

I push the compost
with a tool.
I am making holes
for the seeds.

I get my seeds.
I put one seed in the first
pot and I cover the seed
with compost.

Then I take the next pot.
I make a hole
in the compost
for the seed.

I put one seed in the pot.
I push the seed into the soil
and I cover the seed with
compost.

I make holes for
all the seeds.
I put one seed in every pot
and I push all the seeds
into the soil.
I cover all the seeds
with compost.

Now I am getting
my watering can.
I fill the watering can
with water.

22

I water all the seeds.
The seeds need water –
but I must not give them
too much!

I put the pots
in a bright room.
The seeds need
lots of light.

Now I must wait.
The plants grow
in the light.
I must keep the soil wet.

Now the plants are strong.
I can put them
in my garden.

I dig a hole
in my garden.
I put the plant
in the hole.
I water the plant.

Now all the plants are
in the garden.

I hope they grow strong!
I hope I will see
lots of flowers.

Now it is summer time.
I can see lots of flowers
in my garden!
Good job!

Have you read?

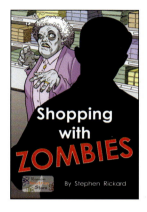

Shopping with Zombies

by Stephen Rickard

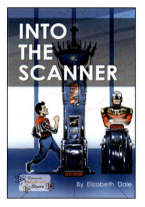

Into the Scanner

by Elizabeth Dale

Have you read?

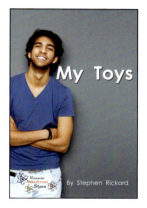

My Toys

by Stephen Rickard

Curry!

by Cath Jones

Ransom Neutron Stars

Planting My Garden
Word count **325**

Red Book Band